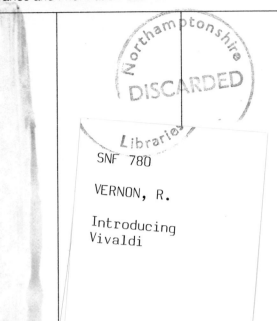

Introducing
VIVALDI

ROLAND VERNON

❧ *Belitha Press*

First published in the UK in 1996 by
   Belitha Press Limited,
   London House, Great Eastern Wharf,
Parkgate Road, London SW11 4NQ

ISBN 1 85561 537 1

British Library Cataloguing in Publication Data
for this book is available from the British Library.

Printed in Hong Kong

Editors: Christine Hatt and Claire Edwards
Designer: Wilson Design Associates
Picture researcher: Diana Morris

Picture acknowledgements: AKG London: front cover l, back
cover, 10t, 11t, 12t, 12b, 13b, 16, 18b, 20, 21, 22t, 28. Bridgeman
Art Library/Ca' Rezzonico, Venice 14b, /Louvre, Paris/Giraudon
15b, 23t, /Palazzo Ducale, Venice 9, /Private Collection 19b,
/Quorini Stampalia Foundation, Venice 8. E.T. Archive/Brera,
Milan 14t, /Museo Correr, Venice 6b, 7, /Museo Civico, Modena
22b, /Museum der Stadt, Vienna 24t, /S. Pietro Maiella
Conservatoire, Naples 26bl, /Quorini Stampalia Foundation,
Venice 19t. Fondazione Giorgio Cini, Venice: 18t. Robert
Harding Picture Library: 6t. Museo Correr, Venice: 10b. Redferns:
29. Scala/Ca' Rezzonico: 27t. Henry Watson Music Library: front
cover, 24b.

CONTENTS

ᶴNTRODUCING VIVALDI

ANTONIO VIVALDI lived and worked in Venice, a rich and beautiful city full of art and music. He wrote vast numbers of works and was one of the most fashionable composers of his day. Apparently, he could compose music faster than a **copyist** could write it out. He was also a brilliant violinist, famous across Europe for his playing. Yet when he died, he and his music were forgotten. Only recently has his name become famous once more. He is now one of the world's favourite composers, with record sales reaching millions. His music is easy to enjoy. It is full of energy, and brings to life for us the elegance of eighteenth-century Venice.

VENICE – A ROMANTIC CITY

There is no city on earth like Venice. It lies in the middle of a huge lagoon on the north-east coast of Italy, surrounded by sea. There are canals instead of roads and boats rather than cars, which give this ancient city a magical, fairy-tale atmosphere. Venice is also full of magnificent palaces, churches, exotic monuments and works of art. These tell us of a rich and powerful history.

Venice was founded in 421 AD, at the time when the Roman Empire was being overrun by invading hordes from central Europe. Villagers from mainland Italy escaped into the mists of the lagoon, where they settled on 118 tiny islands. They began to link up the islands with hundreds of little bridges, and formed the city of Venice, which eventually became an independent **republic**.

Venice today looks much as it did in Vivaldi's time. The Grand Canal, seen here, is the main route through the city.

A view of Venice from above, in about 1600. The many little islands that make up the city are packed full of buildings.

THE DOGE AND PATRICIANS OF VENICE

After the fall of Rome, Venice came under the rule of Byzantium. But from 697 AD, it elected its own ruler, who was called the Doge. During the ninth century, the city became independent and set up a republican style of government. Beneath the Doge, power was held by an elected group of noblemen called the Grand Council. Elections were fair, and no one was allowed to hold too much power. But only those from the best families could stand for election. They were listed in a special Golden Book, and were known as patricians. Ordinary people had no power.

The ruling patricians took part in grand public ceremonies and wore magnificent clothes. Their strict political system involved ruthless police control and the use of spies. People had to ask for special permission even to leave the city. But this style of government kept Venice stable for over 1000 years. The last Doge was **deposed** by **Napoleon** in 1797, and the Venetian Republic came to an end.

The Doge of Venice wore a distinctive style of hat.

During the Middle Ages, Venice became a rich trading port. It acted as a link between Europe and the East. At first merchants traded only salt, but soon began to deal in wine, weapons, jewels, cloth, spices, pepper and many other goods as well. At the same time, Venice also began to build its own powerful navy, which in 1204 captured the great city of **Byzantium** to the east. By the sixteenth century, the Venetian empire had expanded to include parts of Greece, the **Dalmatian Coast**, Crete and Cyprus. Some Venetian merchants travelled far beyond the known world. As a young man, **Marco Polo** (1254–1324) crossed the vast continent of Asia to reach China.

In the seventeenth century, people found other routes to the Far East, and Venice became a less important trading power. But it was still a rich and beautiful city, famous for its art and music. Thousands of tourists, including royalty, visited from all over Europe. Parties, **pageants** and musical galas were organized for them, especially during the **Carnival**. Although no longer a great military power, Venice became Europe's romantic capital, attracting artists and lovers. It is much the same now, and seems almost untouched by the modern world.

St Mark's Square in Venice. St Mark's Basilica, with its domes, can be seen behind the tall bell-tower.

A SICKLY CHILD

*V*enice at the the end of the seventeenth century was not as powerful as it had once been, but it was more famous than ever for its many treasures and festivals. Splendid music was played at every celebration, so there was plenty of work in the city for composers and instrumentalists.

One of the best violinists in Venice was a barber called Giovanni Battista Vivaldi. Although he was only a poor man, he often came into contact with the city's wealthy patricians, because he played in the orchestra of St Mark's **Basilica**. This was one of the best jobs that a musician in Venice could have.

ST MARK'S BASILICA

St Mark's was completed in 1073 and is the most impressive of all Venice's churches. As the Doge's private chapel, it was the heart of religious life in the city. It was built to house the body of the **apostle** St Mark, brought to Venice from Egypt in 828 AD. St Mark's traditional symbol was a lion. This became the **emblem** of the Venetian empire. Over the years, St Mark's Basilica was filled with treasures brought back from conquests abroad.

St Mark's also became an important musical centre. Many composers, including **Gabrieli**, **Monteverdi** and **Cavalli**, wrote their finest music to be performed there. They began to compose a special kind of music for St Mark's, which made use of the church's many galleries and chapels. Groups of musicians played or sang in different places, echoing each other. By Vivaldi's day, there were many other centres of music in Venice, but the grandest festivals still took place in St Mark's.

The winged lion of St Mark, symbol of Venetian power. It can still be seen carved on many old buildings in the city.

Antonio grew up near Venice's **Arsenal**, once the world's most powerful shipyard. Giovanni realized that his son was very musical, and taught him the violin from a young age. Antonio was so talented that he sometimes **deputized** for his father at St Mark's. He also composed, writing at least one piece of church music as a teenager. But Antonio's family thought he would do better in the Church, so in 1693 he began training to become a priest.

On 4 March 1678, Giovanni and his wife Camilla had their first child, a boy named Antonio. He was so weak that they were sure he would not live, so the midwife baptized him straight away. He had a chest illness, which may have been asthma. He survived, but grew into a sickly child and remained weak for the rest of his life.

Ten years later, on 23 March 1703, Antonio was **ordained**. He never worked as a priest, claiming his chest illness made him too weak. However, most people believed he was too interested in music to do other work. Antonio's hair was bright red, like his father's, so he became known as *Il Prete Rosso*, the Red Priest.

Every day, Vivaldi passed Venice's grand Arsenal. Its impressive entrance was like a fortress and big enough for ships to sail through.

A BRILLIANT YOUNG TEACHER

Six months after he was ordained, Vivaldi began a new career as a violin teacher. He was appointed to teach at one of the city's four Ospedali. These were hostels for homeless orphan girls that provided education and musical training, all paid for by the state. Vivaldi's was called the Ospedale della Pietà.

The Pietà was famous for its music. During Vivaldi's time, several of its girls were described as the best instrumentalists and singers in Italy. The girls put on concerts to raise money for the hostel, performing works for orchestra, choir and soloists.

Visiting a convent in eighteenth-century Venice. Girls at the Pietà had to speak to visitors through a grille like this.

These musical evenings at the Pietà became popular tourist attractions, and news of the talented young girls spread far across Europe. Performances were all the more interesting because the girls were half-hidden behind an iron grille. Beautiful music flooded out, but the performers remained a mystery.

In this view of Venice, the Ospedale della Pietà is the large building to the left of the bridge.

Girls from Venice's orphanages perform a concert for Russian royal visitors. The front row play violins, while others sing.

Musicians in those days were treated like servants. As well as teaching, Vivaldi had to make sure all the Pietà's instruments were in good condition. He also had to write a constant stream of new works for the concerts. But he enjoyed working there because he had total control over the way his music was performed. The Pietà was like his own musical workshop.

Vivaldi soon became well known in Venice as a promising young composer, and in 1708 was allowed to deputize for the Pietà's *maestro di coro*, Gasparini. The King of Denmark and Norway attended one of the concerts given at this time and greatly enjoyed the music. Vivaldi took the opportunity to dedicate a set of violin sonatas to him, which were soon published.

We do not know why, but in 1709 Vivaldi was asked to leave the staff of the Pietà. Perhaps the girls were so good at the violin that they no longer needed a teacher. Or perhaps the **governors** were annoyed that Vivaldi was accepting jobs elsewhere.

Francesco Gasparini was the most senior member of the Pietà's music staff when Vivaldi joined.

𝒜 NEW KIND OF MUSIC

𝒱ivaldi's music was new and exciting. It was also distinctive in style. He liked to create vigorous rhythms by using groups of short, repeated notes. This gave his work a feeling of freshness and energy. It was challenging to perform and thrilling to hear. Some solo violin passages were written like complicated exercises, designed to show off the player's skills.

Vivaldi was by now a great **virtuoso** violinist, and visitors to Venice often wrote admiringly about the Red Priest. In 1711, he became famous in the rest of Europe for a new work, *L'Estro Armonico*. This was a set of 12 **concertos** for solo violins and string orchestra that influenced the course of musical history. Published in Holland, it was available all over northern Europe.

An illustration from an early eighteenth-century book on how to play the violin.

A romantic portrait of a violinist-composer, thought to be Vivaldi.

L' ESTRO ARMONICO
Concerti
Consacrati
ALL' ALTEZZA REALE
Di
FERDINANDO III
GRAN PRENCIPE DI TOSCANA
Da D. Antonio Vivaldi
*Musico di Violino e Maestro de Concerti del
Pio Ospidale della Pietà di Venezia*
OPERA TERZA
LIBRO PRIMO.

A Amsterdam
Aux depens D'ESTIENNE ROGER Marchand Libraire
a: Michel Charles Le Cene

The title page of Vivaldi's *L'Estro Armonico*. The publisher, Roger of Amsterdam, was one of the best in Europe.

Vivaldi was a **pioneer** of the concerto. He explored new ways of composing solo instrumental passages to be placed in between sections of orchestral music. This created contrasts in the sound and gave the soloist an opportunity to dazzle the audience. Before Vivaldi, music was more **polyphonic**, which meant that no single part or instrument was more important than another. But after the publication of *L'Estro Armonico*, composers everywhere began to experiment with tuneful solo passages. Instrumentalists then developed personal ways of expressing themselves, and the idea of the musician as **artist** was born. This came to a head in the nineteenth century with the **Romantics**.

Vivaldi's next group of violin concertos was published in 1714, and was called *La Stravaganza*, or 'extravagance'. It was fashionable in Venice at the time for musicians to find new ways to amaze their audiences. Vivaldi's 'extravagance' was suitably adventurous and full of exciting technical surprises.

JOHANN SEBASTIAN BACH (1685–1750)

The great German composer JS Bach was a contemporary of Vivaldi. As a young man, he studied Vivaldi's work and began to write concertos of his own, making use of Italian-style tunes. He also arranged six of Vivaldi's concertos from *L'Estro Armonico* for keyboard. But in many other ways, the lives and music of Bach and Vivaldi were very different. Bach composed in the old-fashioned polyphonic style. He developed ingenious ways of locking musical lines together, using **counterpoint**, **fugues** and **canons**. He was a skilled organist and devout **Lutheran**. Unlike Vivaldi, he never left his own country, and was not interested in personal fame.

Bach wrote vast amounts of music for a variety of instruments, and is now considered one of the greatest composers. But, unlike Vivaldi, he rarely heard his work performed well. He was a gifted teacher and wrote many keyboard pieces for his pupils. The most talented of these were his sons, three of whom became important composers.

Vivaldi probably had no idea he was making musical history. As a working craftsman, he was expected to write music quickly and efficiently. Around 450 of his concertos are known today, but there may be others not yet discovered.

CANALETTO (1697–1768)

The art of painting real places accurately is called topography. The most famous topographical painter in Venice was Giovanni Antonio Canal, known as Canaletto. He produced so many views of Venice that we have a very clear idea of how the city looked during Vivaldi's life. Canaletto's accuracy is almost photographic, and he understood how light changes the appearance of buildings and water. Unlike other artists of the time, he took his easel out into the open to paint from life.

After 1740, fewer tourists visited Venice, because of a war in Europe. Canaletto was invited to England, and stayed there from 1746 to 1755, painting landscapes in his accurate style. His work is like Vivaldi's music in its brilliance and instant appeal.

A painting by Canaletto showing the entrance to St Mark's Square from the Grand Canal. The huge building right of centre is the Doge's palace.

THE LAST YEARS OF THE BAROQUE

Vivaldi's music is full of dramatic contrasts in mood and sound. Exuberance is followed by quietness, solo passages are interrupted by full orchestra, and voices are contrasted with instruments. This gives the music variety and life. It is typical of the artistic era into which Vivaldi was born – the Baroque. Baroque artists aimed to dazzle people. They deliberately broke the existing rules of sculpture, architecture and painting in order to shock and thrill those who saw their work.

Baroque churches were built and decorated to make people feel completely overwhelmed, as if they were close to heaven itself. Artists created a world of glorious make-believe, like the theatre.

This Tiepolo ceiling gives the illusion that the building opens up to heaven.

San Carlo alle Quattro Fontane in Rome, designed by the architect Borromini, is a typical Baroque church.

Painting, sculpture and architecture were used together to create the strongest possible effects. San Carlo alle Quattro Fontane is one of several churches built by the architect Borromini (1599–1667) in Rome. It is a typical Baroque building, with grand swirls, **gilded** decorations, intricate stonework and dramatic paintings around the walls.

By the time Vivaldi was composing, new styles of art were becoming fashionable across Europe. But in Venice the Baroque remained popular. One of the most successful artists of this time was Giovanni Battista Tiepolo (1696–1770). He painted vast **frescoes** that showed a world full of wonder and magnificence. His ceiling frescoes gave the impression that heaven was opening up above the building. This use of **illusion** was a typically theatrical Baroque trick. Like Venetian music, Tiepolo's splendid paintings showed the city's great wealth and dignity to both residents and visitors.

The huge tourist trade in Venice at this time also created a new fashion in art. Visitors wanted to take home a memento of the city and its islands. Painters such as Guardi (1712–1793) and Canaletto began to paint souvenir landscapes. They show Venice bathed in bright, clear sunlight that shimmers and glistens on the water.

Francesco Guardi's painting of the Doge's barge, the Bucintoro. The barge is surrounded by small boats called gondolas.

Vivaldi set a fine example to his pupils, performing much of his own work at the Pietà concerts.

CHURCH SPLENDOUR

*V*ivaldi returned to the Pietà, as violin teacher, in September 1711. He worked for the Pietà, on and off, for nearly 40 years. Every so often his job was taken away. We do not know why, but perhaps he had enemies who plotted against him, or perhaps the patricians did not like to see his rise from poverty to international fame. Vivaldi was also a very good businessman, and he may have annoyed his employers by asking for more money too often.

Vivaldi at the height of his career as a busy composer with several jobs.

The governors of the Pietà had to admit that the Red Priest was providing them with exciting music and an excellent reputation. In 1713, when their *maestro di coro*, Gasparini, resigned, Vivaldi was put in charge of composing the Pietà's church music. He was asked to write two **masses** and two **settings** of **vespers** every year. He also had to produce two **motets** every month, and any other music the Pietà might need for its religious festivals.

Vivaldi's church and choral music was as brilliant as his instrumental pieces. Works such as his famous **Gloria** had an immediate appeal. They were exuberant and grand, just like Baroque art. The young girls of the Pietà must have greatly enjoyed performing music that was so electrifying. These church works also express a deep respect for the power of God, especially in their slower and quieter moments. Although he never worked as a priest, Vivaldi was a very religious man.

St Mark's was the most spectacular place to hear Venetian church music. Inside are beautiful mosaics, patterned marble floors and treasures built into the walls.

In May 1716, Vivaldi's job at the Pietà changed again. He became *maestro di concerti* – director of instrumental music. This meant he was no longer just a teacher, but a respected musical figure.

But by this time, Vivaldi had developed another great interest. He had begun to compose a different kind of music that was becoming highly fashionable in Venice. This music was **opera**.

THE BUSY IMPRESARIO

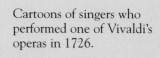

*W*hen he was not working at the Pietà, Vivaldi began composing for the theatre. He probably joined his father in playing for the orchestra of the **Teatro San Angelo**. The people of Venice were passionate about opera. Their enthusiasm became a craze in 1709, when the great German composer Handel visited the city with his latest opera, *Agrippina*. Vivaldi realized that he could make money from writing operas, and took a month's leave in 1713 to start composing one. It was called *Ottone in Villa*, and was first produced with great success in the nearby city of Vicenza.

Members of the audience at an eighteenth-century opera often walked around, paying very little attention to what was happening on stage. Perhaps that is why they did not mind if the music was not particularly special or original.

OPERA IN VENICE

The world's first composer of opera, Claudio Monteverdi (1567–1643), spent the later part of his life in Venice. His masterpiece, *L'Incoronazione di Poppea*, was produced there in 1642. From this time on, opera became the most popular form of entertainment in Venice. The first public opera house in the world was built there in 1637.

Opera combined everything Venetians most enjoyed: music, grand spectacle and drama. Almost all the **plots** were taken from ancient Greek and Roman stories. Gods and heroes were brought to life and wondrous legends set to music. A fantastic world of make-believe was created, using stage machinery, lighting effects and even live animals.

An eighteenth-century audience behaved very differently from a modern audience. During a performance they chatted, smoked, played cards, gambled and ate supper. They went to the opera for light entertainment, dazzling sights and to meet friends.

The Carnival was an important season in Venice, especially for opera and music. It stretched from 26 December to 30 March and was completely dedicated to pleasure. There were many grand parties and everyone wore masks. This gave people more freedom to do as they liked. Patricians and commoners mixed together, lovers met openly and musicians paraded noisily around the streets. Some carnival-goers even threw eggs and bottles from windows. Foreign tourists were very attracted to all this fun and freedom. The Carnival still takes place today, but is shorter and less wild.

From then on, Vivaldi became an important person in the Venetian opera world. The city had many theatres and there was a constant demand for new operas. Composers had to write them extremely quickly and in large quantities. Vivaldi wrote one of his operas, *Tito Manlio*, in just five days. In total, he claimed that he wrote 94 operas, although today we only know of around 50. This is a huge number, especially as Vivaldi was writing and performing so much other music at the same time.

Many Venetian operas from this period sound similar. This is partly because composers borrowed each other's tunes, or used music from their own past works. The music was less important to audiences than the chance of hearing their favourite stars sing show-pieces. Sometimes singers completely changed a composer's music to suit themselves and please the audience.

Vivaldi was not happy with this situation. He became the resident **impresario** at the Teatro San Angelo to make sure his own work was properly performed. This was a huge job. He had to compose operas, hire singers, sell tickets and generally manage the company. There was less time than ever for his Pietà work.

The German-born composer George Frideric Handel (1685–1759) became famous all over Europe for his operas.

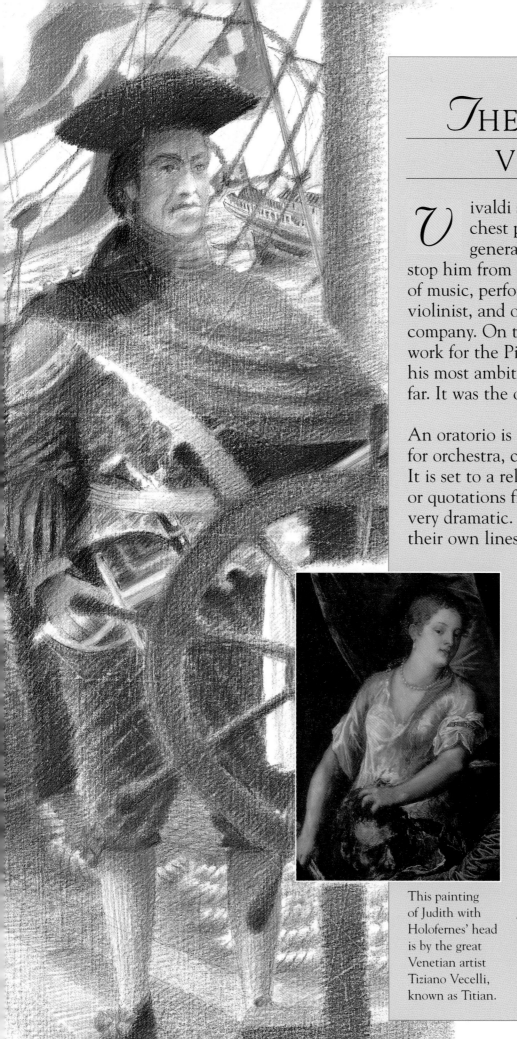

THE MUSIC OF VICTORY

*V*ivaldi suffered all his life from chest pains, breathlessness and general tiredness. But this did not stop him from composing a vast amount of music, performing superbly as a solo violinist, and organizing an entire opera company. On top of this, he continued to work for the Pietà. In 1716, he produced his most ambitious project for the girls so far. It was the oratorio *Juditha Triumphans*.

An oratorio is a large-scale piece of music for orchestra, choir and several soloists. It is set to a religious text, usually poetry or quotations from the Bible. Oratorios are very dramatic. Different characters have their own lines to sing, rather like opera, but with no acting. *Juditha* was Vivaldi's second oratorio. He composed it for the Pietà, to commemorate an important event.

In the summer of 1716, Venice was at war with Turkey. The focus of the war was the island of Corfu, an important base of Venetian power in the **Adriatic Sea**. The people of Venice saw the war as an opportunity to restore their empire to its former glory. Vivaldi wrote *Juditha Triumphans* to stir up patriotism in the city by comparing the conflict to the story of Judith and Holofernes in the Bible.

This painting of Judith with Holofernes' head is by the great Venetian artist Tiziano Vecelli, known as Titian.

VENICE BATTLES AGAINST TURKEY

The Venetian Republic struggled hard to keep hold of its empire and its trading power. This led to many wars with the other great empire of the **Mediterranean** – Turkey. In 1645 the Turks laid siege to the island of Crete, which then belonged to Venice. The siege lasted 22 years and thousands died before the Turks won control of the island. In the 1680s, Venice regained a little power when it joined an alliance of nations called the Holy League. The League was set up to prevent Turkey from expanding into Europe. But most of the lands it won went to Austria and Russia, the strongest countries in the alliance. Venice held on to Corfu in 1716, but lost many other territories in the final peace treaty (the Treaty of Passarowitz) in 1718. This marked the end of Venice's time as a great imperial power.

The Doge and his Grand Council meet to discuss one of Venice's many wars.

In the story, Judith saves her people from invaders by beheading Holofernes, the enemy general, while he sleeps. In Vivaldi's oratorio, Judith represents Venice, and Holofernes the Turkish **sultan**. By the time the work was first performed, in November 1716, Venice had finally defeated the Turks in Corfu, and the whole city was celebrating victory.

Vivaldi used as many musicians and types of instrument as he could in this oratorio. It was full of contrasting effects and different combinations of singers and instruments. He made it the grandest work that he had ever written for the Pietà.

BEYOND VENICE

$\mathscr{I}$n 1718, Vivaldi was offered a job in the city of Mantua, about 120 kilometres west of Venice. Mantua was ruled by Austria, and its governor was Prince Philip of Hesse-Darmstadt. For three years, Vivaldi worked as one of Prince Philip's court musicians, composing mainly **secular** instrumental works. He left Mantua in 1720, but continued to write music for the prince, sending it by post.

In Mantua, Vivaldi also produced more operas. His fame had now spread beyond Venice, and he was asked to compose operas for other cities as well, such as Florence, Milan and Munich. He travelled to these cities as often as he could to make sure that his works were being performed as he had written them.

Pier Leone Ghezzi's sketch of Vivaldi. It is almost a cartoon, but cartoons often say more about a person than paintings.

The palace in Mantua where Vivaldi served as court musician. While away from Venice, he mixed with a number of rich aristocrats.

People in Rome enjoyed grand musical events. This picture shows a spectacular concert put on there in 1758.

After leaving Mantua, Vivaldi made three trips to Rome to put on new operas. One of his grandest patrons there was Pietro Ottobini, a **cardinal** who loved music and surrounded himself with composers and artists. One of Ottobini's friends was the painter Pier Leone Ghezzi. His sketch of Vivaldi is the only definite likeness of the composer in existence.

Vivaldi became as famous in Rome for his violin-playing as for his popular operas. He often wrote passages for solo violin in the operas, so that he could dazzle the audience with his great skill.

The people of Rome adored Vivaldi and his vibrant music. He was twice invited to the **Vatican** to play for the pope. As a priest, Vivaldi felt especially honoured to have the opportunity of performing for the head of the Church.

The governors of the Pietà were not happy that their *maestro* was so often absent. They eventually agreed that he should write two works for them every month. If he was away from Venice, he was allowed to send them by post. Vivaldi was now the Pietà's visiting celebrity composer, rather than a regular member of its music staff.

TRAVELS AND SCANDALS

*V*ivaldi published a set of concertos in 1725 that brought him even greater success. It was called *The Contest between Harmony and Invention*, and included a group of four concertos, *The Four Seasons*. These have become one of the most popular musical works of all time. Vivaldi published two more sets of concertos between 1729 and 1730, before discovering he could make more money by selling his manuscripts than by having them published.

Vivaldi travelled Europe during his later years. Carriages were uncomfortable and there was a risk of bandits.

THE FOUR SEASONS

This remarkable work is made up of four concertos, named after the year's four seasons: spring, summer, autumn and winter. Each individual season is described through a musical story. The printed **score** of *The Four Seasons* begins with four poems, probably written by Vivaldi, which tell the same stories in words. The score also includes instructions for the musicians. At one point in *Spring*, for example, Vivaldi writes: 'the dog barking'. This tells the string players they have reached the point in the story where a sleeping goatherd is guarded by his faithful dog on a sunny spring afternoon. These works show how sensitive Vivaldi was to the natural world. No other composer had ever attempted to describe nature as accurately as this. The concertos also include wonderful pieces for the solo violinist, which Vivaldi wrote, of course, for himself.

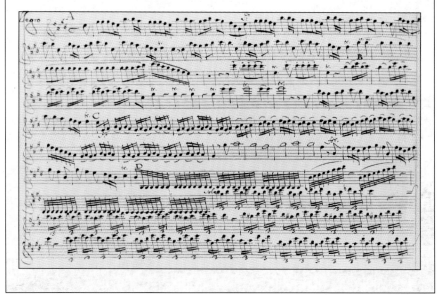

By now it was well known in Venice that the Red Priest was living with a woman. She was Anna Giraud, a Mantuan opera singer who often starred in Vivaldi's productions. She was also his pupil and sang at the Pietà, but audiences praised her acting and good looks more often than her voice. She was about 30 years younger than the composer and accompanied him on his travels.

Catholic priests are not allowed to marry, so Vivaldi claimed that he and Anna were just friends. But Venetians enjoyed gossip and scandal. A rumour started that Vivaldi and his favourite singer were lovers, and it quickly spread around the city.

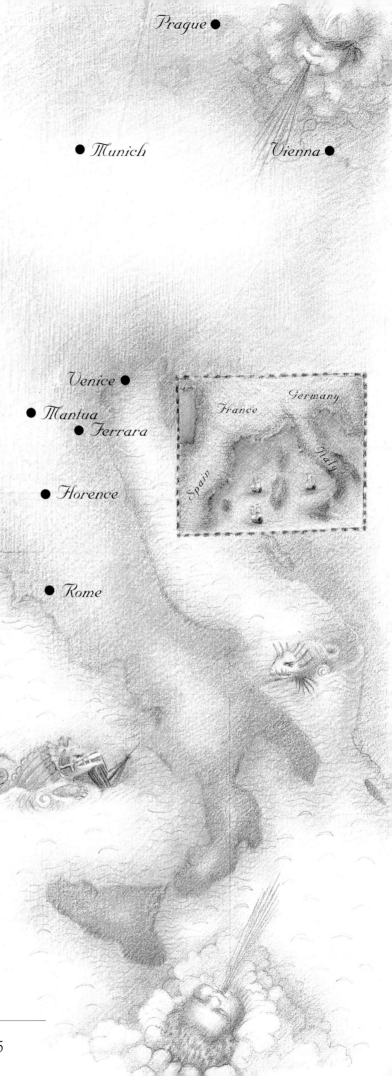

In 1729, Vivaldi set out with his father on a trip to Germany and did not return to Venice until 1733. During this time he probably also visited Vienna and Prague to direct his operas. From 1735 onwards he was constantly in and out of Venice, crossing the lagoon to organize opera seasons on the mainland.

In 1737, the city of Ferrara was about to host one of these seasons, when Vivaldi received a blow. The Archbishop of Ferrara, Tommaso Ruffo, refused to let him into the city to direct his opera. The main reason the archbishop gave was Vivaldi's relationship with Anna. It was a stern act and Vivaldi felt crushed.

Tommaso Ruffo, Archbishop of Ferrara, punished Vivaldi. He thought the composer set a bad example to other priests.

We know little about where Vivaldi went, or for how long. The map (right) shows some cities he definitely visited.

A CHANGE OF FASHION

Vivaldi wrote popular music. He wanted to entertain audiences rather than express himself in some deep or personal way. But as time went by, he grew more and more out of touch with fashion in Venice. People's musical taste at this time was influenced by a witty nobleman and composer called Benedetto Marcello. In 1720, Marcello wrote a book called *Il Teatro alla Moda* (Fashionable Theatre), which made fun of all the operatic **conventions** of the day.

The title page of *Il Teatro alla Moda*. After this amusing book was published, Vivaldi's reputation as an opera composer declined in Venice and never properly recovered.

In his book, Marcello wrote that the music in the operas was poor and the drama pathetically weak. He particularly mocked a composer he called Aldaviva – an obvious reference to Vivaldi. The book's title page also showed a drawing of a little dancing angel wearing a priest's hat and playing the violin – another joke at the fashionable Red Priest's expense.

Benedetto Marcello (1686–1739) was one of the most interesting and talented men in Venice. He composed music, played the violin and wrote books. He was also a lawyer and a member of a patrician family.

This banqueting scene from eighteenth-century Venice shows how splendidly the city entertained its visitors. The 1740 royal visit for which Vivaldi organized a concert would have been just as magnificent.

Il Teatro alla Moda went on to make fun of the grovelling dedications that Vivaldi put at the beginning of his musical works. Marcello imitated his style and included an exaggeratedly humble dedication, in which a composer says he is not worthy to kiss the flea bites on his patron's dog.

When this book was published, the people of Venice suddenly decided they wanted to listen to a different kind of opera, and gradually Vivaldi became a less popular composer. He did not write another opera in Venice for over four years.

Audiences abroad still liked Vivaldi's work, which is why he began to travel so much. But in 1739, a visitor to Venice wrote that although Vivaldi still composed great quantities of music, he was no longer much admired in the city. Fashion had changed, and people were bored with him.

Vivaldi scored one final triumph at the Pietà with a grand gala concert, which celebrated a royal visit in March 1740. Then he decided it was time to leave Venice for good. He began raising money for what would be his last journey.

FORGOTTEN FOR TWO CENTURIES

*V*ivaldi left Venice in May 1740, bound for Vienna, capital of the Austrian Empire. He probably hoped to be offered work at the court of the emperor, Charles VI. Charles had met Vivaldi in 1728 and particularly liked his music. He had made the composer a knight of the empire and presented him with a golden chain. But Charles died unexpectedly in October 1740, after eating some poisonous mushrooms, and Vivaldi's hopes of a job at the court died with him.

Vivaldi had fallen a long way since the days when his music was the glory of Venice. He was a forgotten composer in a foreign city with no money. For many years no one knew when, where or how the composer died. But in 1938, a Viennese register of burials was discovered, showing that Vivaldi died of an 'internal inflammation' and was buried on 28 July 1741. His unmarked grave now lies beneath a busy road in the city. He died a **pauper**.

Charles VI (1685–1740), emperor of the Austrians, also had the title Holy Roman Emperor. He was perhaps the most powerful ruler in Europe.

Fashionable new composers quickly took Vivaldi's place in Venice. He was soon forgotten even in his own city. For 200 years, only a few musical historians knew of him. He was just an obscure composer of some music that had been rearranged by the great Bach. Then, in 1926, an extraordinary discovery took place. Several volumes of Vivaldi's music were found in a monastery in Italy – part of the long-lost library of an old patrician family. In 1930, the other half of the library was tracked down.

Vivaldi's brilliance was rediscovered. The first festival of his music took place in 1939. In 1950, the first recording of *The Four Seasons* was released. Since then, there have been over 150 more, including a chart-topping version by the young British violinist Nigel Kennedy. Vivaldi is now established as one of the great composers of the Baroque.

Nigel Kennedy's style makes classical music attractive to young people.

TIME CHART

1678   Antonio Vivaldi born in Venice, 4 March.

1693   Begins training for the priesthood, 18 September.

1703   Ordained priest, 23 March.
Appointed violin teacher at the Ospedale della Pietà in September.

1705   First music published.

1708   King of Denmark and Norway visits the Pietà. Vivaldi dedicates violin sonatas to him, early 1709.

1709   Leaves staff of the Pietà, 24 February.

1711   Reappointed as violin teacher at the Pietà, 27 September.
L'Estro Armonico, Vivaldi's first set of concertos, published.

1713   *Ottone in Villa*, Vivaldi's first opera, performed in Vicenza, 17 March.
Gasparini leaves the Pietà in April. Vivaldi becomes chief composer.

1714   Becomes impresario at Teatro San Angelo.
Publishes group of violin concertos called *La Stravaganza*.

1716   Appointed *maestro di concerti* at the Pietà, 24 May.
Venice battles with Turkey over Corfu.
First performance of oratorio *Juditha Triumphans*, November.

1718   Begins working for Prince Philip of Hesse-Darmstadt in Mantua.
Probably meets Anna Giraud.

1720   Returns to Venice from Mantua, December.
Benedetto Marcello's book *Il Teatro alla Moda* published in Venice.

1723   Becomes visiting celebrity composer for the Pietà, July.
Visits Rome (also in 1724) and meets the pope.

1725   *The Contest between Harmony and Invention*, including *The Four Seasons*, published in December.

1728   Meets Austrian emperor, Charles VI, in September.

1729   Sets out for northern Europe in November (returns to Venice 1733).

1735   Reappointed *maestro di concerti* at the Pietà, 5 August.

1737   Cardinal Ruffo forbids Vivaldi to enter Ferrara, 16 November.

1740   Musical gala at the Pietà to mark a royal visit, 21 March.
Resigns post at the Pietà in May and leaves Venice for Austria.

1741   Antonio Vivaldi dies and is buried in Vienna on 28 July.

GLOSSARY

Adriatic Sea the part of the Mediterranean Sea that stretches all the way down the eastern coast of Italy, southwards to Greece. (See Dalmatian Coast.)

apostle one of the 12 disciples chosen by Jesus to teach Christianity.

Arsenal a place where army and navy equipment is built. Arsenals are also used to store weapons and ammunition.

artist this word does not always mean a painter – it can also refer to a musician who performs with a great deal of expression.

Basilica a word used in Roman times to describe a hall or large public building. Christians later called their large churches 'basilicas'.

Byzantium the capital of the Roman Empire from 330 AD. The city was later called Constantinople, and is now known as Istanbul, in Turkey.

canon piece of music in which one voice or instrument begins with a single tune, a second joins in with the same tune a short time later, then a third and so on. Although all the parts in a canon play the same music, they are all at a different stage at any particular time. (See fugue.)

cardinal a very senior priest in the Roman Catholic Church. When the pope dies, it is the cardinals' responsibility to elect a new pope.

Carnival a carnival is traditionally a time of celebration before the beginning of Lent, the 40-day period leading up to Easter. The Venice Carnival was a unique and special celebration.

Cavalli, Francesco (1602–1676) Italian composer and important pioneer of opera. He sang as a boy in the choir at St Mark's Basilica, Venice, and later worked there as director of music.

concerto piece of music written for orchestra and solo instruments.

conventions the styles, habits or fashions of certain periods in history. Conventions can become almost like rules.

copyist a person who copies out a composer's manuscript neatly, so that it can be read by performers.

counterpoint a musical line written or played alongside another of equal importance. (See polyphonic.)

Dalmatian Coast the coastline of the land on the opposite side of the Adriatic Sea to Italy. Dalmatia is a region in Croatia. (See Adriatic Sea.)

deposed removed from power.

deputized stood in or substituted for.

emblem an object used as a symbol. Emblems can be seen on flags, signs, coats-of-arms or buildings.

frescoes paintings done straight on to wet wall plaster.

fugue piece of music in which the opening tune is repeated by each new voice or instrument as it joins in. Unlike the tune of a canon, which remains the same for all the parts throughout, the tune of each voice or instrument in a fugue develops separately, so that eventually several different tunes, all based on the same original, interweave. (See canon.)

Gabrieli, Giovanni (about 1556–1612) Venetian composer who worked for much of his life as the organist of St Mark's Church. His uncle, Andrea Gabrieli, was also a famous Venetian composer, and they both wrote magnificent church music to be performed at St Mark's.

gilded painted or covered with gold leaf.

Gloria a part of the Christian mass, which is often set to music by composers. (See mass.)

governors the group of directors at a school or college.

illusion something that seems real but is not. Artists often use illusion to make viewers feel that they are looking at a real scene, when they are in fact only looking at a painting.

impresario someone who organizes grand musical events.

Lutheran a member of the Church founded by Martin Luther (1483–1546). Luther was an important German religious reformer who broke away from the Roman Catholic Church in 1517.

maestro di coro this is Italian for director of the choir, but at the Pietà, the *maestro di coro* was the most senior musician on the staff.

mass an important part of church worship in the Christian religion. Many composers have set the mass to music.

Mediterranean the sea in southern Europe that is almost enclosed by land. It divides Europe from Africa, and stretches between Spain in the west and Turkey in the east.

Monteverdi, Claudio (1567–1643) Italian composer and pioneer of opera, who also worked as director of music at St Mark's Church. He invented new ways of composing and greatly influenced the history of music.

motet piece of church music written for a choir.

Napoleon (1769–1821) Emperor of France from 1804 to 1814. Born on the island of Corsica, he became a famous general while still young, and began ruling France in 1799. After fighting wars all across Europe, he was finally defeated at the Battle of Waterloo in 1815. Napoleon was exiled for the rest of his life to St Helena, a small island in the Atlantic Ocean.

opera a musical drama in which the performers sing most or all of their lines, usually accompanied by an orchestra. In an opera, the music is just as important as the words.

ordained when a man or woman is ordained, he or she goes through a special church ceremony to become a priest.

pageant spectacular public event, usually involving grand processions and drama in which people dress up in historical costumes.

pauper a very poor person.

pioneer a person who prepares the way for others, such as an explorer, inventor, or someone with new ideas.

plots the stories of plays, books or operas.

Polo, Marco (1254–1324) Venetian merchant and traveller who spent 17 years of his life in China and also journeyed to many other countries.

polyphonic used to describe music that has several musical lines of equal importance weaving around each other at the same time, rather than one main tune line. (See counterpoint.)

republic a country that is governed by the people or on behalf of the people by others they have elected. A republic is not ruled by a king, queen, emperor or other ruler who has simply inherited power from a parent or other relative.

Romantics artists, writers and musicians of the late eighteenth and early nineteenth centuries who were fascinated by nature, loneliness and individual expression.

score the complete written or printed manuscript of a piece of music.

secular non-religious, or belonging to the world outside the Church.

setting musical arrangement of certain words or texts. The words are 'set' to music.

sultan a king, prince or ruler in a Muslim country such as Turkey in the eighteenth century.

Teatro San Angelo one of the many theatres in Venice where operas were performed.

Vatican an area in Rome where the pope lives. The Vatican is the centre of the Roman Catholic Church. Within the Vatican are the Sistine Chapel and St Peter's Church.

vespers an evening service of worship in the Christian religion.

virtuoso a particularly skilful performer who has mastered all the techniques of playing his or her chosen instrument.

INDEX